A SEARCH
◇ FOR ◇

CHARIS-
MATIC

Reality

A SEARCH ◇ FOR ◇

CHARIS-MATIC

Reality

ONE
◇ MAN'S ◇
PILGRIMAGE

NEIL BABCOX

MULTNOMAH PRESS
PORTLAND, OREGON 97266

Edited by Liz Heaney and Jane Aldrich Franks
Cover design and illustration by Larry Ulmer

A SEARCH FOR CHARISMATIC REALITY
© 1985 by Multnomah Press
Portland, Oregon 97266

Printed in the United States of America

Library of Congress Cataloging in Publication Data

Babcox, Neil.
  A search for charismatic reality.

  Includes bibliographies.
    1. Glossolalia—Controversial literature.
2. Prophecy (Christianity)—Controversial literature.
3. Babcox, Neil.   I. Title.
BT122.5.B33   1985   234'.13   84-25506
ISBN 0-88070-085-8

85 86 87 88 89 90 91 – 10 9 8 7 6 5 4 3 2 1

Contents

Foreword

This book is not for the insincere or dishonest. It is for those who earnestly search for spiritual reality. It is the result of the honest and fruitful search of a charismatic pastor for the reality of Christ in and through the gift of tongues.

The reader will thrill with the writer's sincere quest to discover the roots of reality in his own charismatic experience. It is one of the most exciting testimonies of genuine spiritual thirst for biblical truth I have ever read.

The heart of this book brings one to the depth of the charismatic experience and to the heart of God. It is a difficult book to put down before you finish it.

Both non-charismatic and charismatic readers will identify with the message in these pages. Like no other book I know, this one bridges the gulf between these two groups in an irenic and unprecedented way.

The approach is sensitive and informed. The message is crucial and the style is eminently readable. The impact on readers will be both enriching and enlightening.

Foreword

Within its own compass it answers better than any book available the question of the biblical basis and spiritual reality of the charismatic gifts.

Norman L. Geisler

To the Reader

Socrates said that the unexamined life is not worth living. I would add that the unexamined faith is not worth believing. Our strongest convictions, our most cherished experiences, can withstand even the closest scrutiny if they are grounded in the truth of God. I have written this book for those who have the courage to examine their faith, though the process of doing so may prove to be disturbing.

Those in search of "proof-texts" or theological profundities will be disappointed, for this book is not the product of abstract, theological reflection, but of inner conflict. To such doctrines as the finality of God's revelation in Christ, the foundational character of the apostolic testimony, the nature of miracles in the redemptive purposes of God, and the authority and sufficiency of Scripture for faith and life, I have nothing to add except my own testimony.

My testimony is this: I have come to believe that certain experiences of mine related to such spiritual gifts as speaking in tongues and prophecy were not authentic. This book is the record of the struggles that led me to adopt this conclusion. My hope is

To the Reader

that others who are undergoing similar struggles may benefit by my experiences. Longfellow wrote, "Sometimes we may learn more from a man's errors than from his virtues." I invite all who take this book in hand to learn from my errors.

O for a Thousand Tongues 1

Sometimes prayer can get you into trouble—believe me, I know. One prayer that can be particularly troublesome is, "Lord, show me the truth and I'll stand by it and affirm it no matter what the consequences." This book is one of those consequences.

It all began when a university professor, a Christian, spoke the following words to me at a prayer meeting: "Why that's nothing more than gibberish." He was referring to speaking in tongues, and I was appalled. "That's positively irreverent," I muttered to myself. I guess he just didn't appreciate what speaking in tongues meant to me, and what I had to go through to receive the gift.

I might never have come to church if it were not for people speaking in tongues. I was raised in a non-Christian home, and had never heard the gospel until I enrolled in college at the age of eighteen. It's not that my parents were hostile to the gospel; the subject just never came up. But the summer before I left home for Southern Illinois University, Pat, who would later become my sister-in-law, told me about a prayer meeting where people were speaking in tongues.

"Speaking in tongues? What on earth is that?"

"It's mentioned in the Bible," she answered. "It's people speaking unknown languages by the power of God."

My initial reaction to speaking in tongues was like the multitude's on the day of Pentecost: "Amazed and perplexed, they asked one another, 'What does this mean?'" (Acts 2:12). I shared their bewilderment, for not only had I never heard of speaking in tongues, I had never heard of the power of God. My curiosity, however, was aroused.

"Why don't you come to the meeting tonight?" Pat asked. "Brother Bernardi is going to be there. He's wonderful. He can pray for you and then you can speak in tongues."

"I can?"

It is difficult to describe how bizarre that prayer meeting was. It was held at a plush house in Long Grove, Illinois. The hostess, in her flowing, powder blue gown, fluttered about like Tinkerbell welcoming her guests. Her greetings were friendly, to say the least. In fact, they were too friendly— her exuberant hugs and kisses embarrassed me.

As the meeting began, it occurred to me that there was something distinctly eerie about our silver-haired hostess. Later I discovered she was a spiritualist. She made quite a striking picture, seated in her ornately carved chair and sipping red wine from a long-stemmed glass. Her husband, wearing a three-piece suit and a bemused expression, occasionally strolled through our midst on his way to the kitchen to refill his glass. I noticed the featured speaker, Brother Bernardi, sitting in a corner of the living room with a grave look on his face. He seemed to be at a loss as to how to appraise the situation.

When it was time to pray, the lights were dimmed. We joined hands and waited silently for several minutes. Everyone began praying simultaneously. There was something about the way they prayed—the tone or pitch of their voices—that I have come to recognize since then. Perhaps the best way to describe it is to call it a sort of desperate enthusiasm. Spontaneously, the praying subsided to a hush. The room was charged with anticipation when, finally, someone began speaking in tongues. Truthfully, I was scared. Scared but impressed. After a burst of excited praise, somebody said, "God wants to give someone in this room the gift of tongues."

"Who? Me?" I thought with horror.

Everyone crowded around me in a circle. They placed their hands on me and prayed in tongues. Brother Bernardi urged me to speak out by faith. But I just couldn't bring myself to do it—which isn't surprising when you consider that I wasn't a Christian, not to mention that I hadn't the dimmest notion of what was going on.

Of course, this was by no means a typical charismatic prayer meeting. Far from it! But nevertheless, it was because of this unusual prayer meeting that I became interested not only in the gift of tongues, but in the Bible and in Christianity. The hymn writer said, "God works in a mysterious way His wonders to perform." I have to add a hearty "amen" to that.

Not long after that prayer meeting, I left home to attend Southern Illinois University. And being the practical-minded person that I am, I decided to major in philosophy. I really don't know why I was attracted to philosophy except to say that after a life of underachieving and doing poorly in school, I experienced a genuine intellectual awakening.

I remember one incident that occurred a few months into my first semester. I was walking down a back road when a very decrepit-looking wino ambled up to me. His chin was covered with gray stubble and he was carrying a bottle of cheap wine in a brown paper bag.

"Hey boy, just what are you studying over there at that school?" he asked in an undisguised tone of contempt.

O for a Thousand Tongues

"Well," I said, clearing my throat, "I'm studying philosophy."

"Don't you mean 'fool-osophy?'" He laughed and took a slug of wine. I must confess that ever since I have been a little hesitant about admitting I majored in philosophy.

Southern Illinois University is a large state school with an enrollment of over twenty thousand students. When I attended in the early seventies, the campus was filled with demonstrations, tear gas, hippies, and Jesus people. The Jesus people combed the streets in droves playing their guitars, handing out evangelistic tracts and newspapers, and telling people, "Jesus loves you." In those days it was kind of hard *not* to hear the gospel.

One of the first of the Jesus people that I chanced to meet was a rather foreboding looking fellow. His long black hair was parted in the middle and hung half way down the back of his black leather jacket. Peering at me through his round, wire-rimmed glasses, he asked if I knew that Jesus loved me and had died for my sins. I replied that I had heard something to that effect and we had a friendly discussion about it. But before leaving, I asked a question: "Have you ever heard of speaking in tongues?" Sure enough, he had, and he went on to explain that I could see for myself

18

at one of their meetings. That was all I needed to hear.

Soon I began attending a Bible study and a prayer meeting. The Bible study was about unfulfilled prophecy and was based upon Hal Lindsay's book, *The Late Great Planet Earth*. I'm afraid I was something of a sore spot at those meetings. No one ever explained to me you weren't supposed to smoke at a Bible study! However, it didn't take me too long to figure that out.

I can't say precisely when I was saved; only that it was over a period of several months. I wanted desperately to have the peace with God everyone spoke about, but it seemed to elude me. People kept saying Jesus lived in their hearts, but this seemed too subjective, based as it was upon personal experience. The big question that came to consume my soul was, how can I know if Jesus lives in my heart? I went through a tremendous inner struggle about the assurance of salvation, and without going into the details of that struggle, let me just say that when I finally realized I was a sinner, that I was undeserving of God's grace, and that salvation was a free gift based upon the merits of Jesus Christ, the assurance came. But first I had to take my eyes off my own experience and focus them long and hard upon the Son of God. I learned my inheritance was reserved for me in heaven—not in my heart. And there it is

19

protected by God's almighty power (1 Peter 1:4, 5).

Despite the fact that I had found my assurance in Christ, I still felt there was something missing: I didn't speak in tongues as everybody else did. Furthermore, my spiritual life was very unsatisfactory to me. It was like a roller coaster: it went up and down and all around. Noticing my discouragement, friends said, "Neil, you need to be baptized with the Holy Spirit. Don't stop short with salvation," they would say, "but be filled with the Holy Spirit and then you will be able to live the victorious life. God will give you a new language which you can use to praise Him." As a result I went through another tremendous struggle. Only this time it revolved around receiving the gift of tongues rather than attaining assurance.

And so I prayed and I prayed. "O God, I want everything you have to give me. I want to be filled with your Holy Spirit. I want to praise you in a new language. Please hear my prayer." But the heavens were brass. No matter how much I asked, I just didn't seem to have the faith to receive. Many times I asked others to pray for me. I wanted them to lay hands on me the way Paul laid his hands on the Ephesians. But all of this was to no avail. I think I was becoming something of a proverb: "Brother Neil doesn't speak in tongues yet, but, oh boy, when he does . . ."

O for a Thousand Tongues

Finally I did; and not surprisingly, it happened at another prayer meeting. By this time I was desperate. I was just waiting for those magic words to be spoken one more time: "God wants to give someone in this room the gift of tongues." Should those words be spoken, I surmised, in all probability they would refer to me. This was not particularly astute, considering that I was the only one left who didn't speak in tongues! And sure enough, someone said it.

As the people started forming a circle around me, I thought about the dynamic experience of the disciples on the day of Pentecost. I also thought about the many testimonies I had heard. "It's the power of God within—like electricity." "It's the love of God being shed abroad in your heart." "It's like being a giant taste bud in an ocean of honey." Would one of these experiences be mine?

The people prayed but nothing happened. "Please, God, please," I thought. They continued to pray, but still nothing happened. My heart seemed dead and cold. "Oh God, why can't I be like these other Christians?" After ten minutes or so, everyone in the room was getting discouraged. Finally, one brother spoke up. "Neil, God loves you, but you have to speak out. You must initiate it. Begin to utter something now or you'll never receive it." I hung my head in shame. Hot tears began to stream down my cheeks.

21

O for a Thousand Tongues

"Okay," I sobbed, "This is it." And with trembling lips I managed to choke out a few incomprehensible syllables.

"That's it, Neil. You've got it!"

At first I was somewhat uneasy about this experience. But as I walked home and tried to speak in tongues again, I found that I could do so much more fluently. As I lay in bed that night I began to thank God. I spoke to Him for a long while in my new-found language. Soon it almost seemed to be second nature. My heart was overjoyed. "At last!" I thought, "God has answered my prayers."

Speaking in tongues was a very rewarding experience for me. Every day I spent a large portion of my prayer time speaking in tongues. I felt that I was speaking mysteries to God through the Holy Spirit (1 Corinthians 14:2). I felt that the Holy Spirit was interceding for me with groanings too deep to be uttered (Romans 8:26, 27). I liked to imagine that the Holy Spirit was using me to pray for someone in trouble—perhaps a missionary in some far off land. Whenever there was an urgent prayer request, such as if a

O for a Thousand Tongues

friend were hospitalized, I would pray in tongues. "Surely the most effective way to pray is to let the Holy Spirit pray through me," I reasoned. It was comforting to think that even if I didn't know how to pray, the Holy Spirit did.

Speaking in tongues seemed to enrich our public meetings, too. When I spoke a message in tongues at a prayer meeting or Bible study, someone else would interpret it. When this happened, we all felt God was speaking to us. We thought this meant God cared about us in particular and had given this gift to encourage and edify us. We also sang in tongues. And when everyone sang in tongues in unison, it sounded to me like a heavenly choir. I felt that I knew what Paul meant when he said, "I thank God I speak in tongues more than all of you" (1 Corinthians 14:18).

It was just around this time—at the peak of my joy—that the professor said to me, "Gibberish. That's nothing more than gibberish." I was shocked. How could he say such a thing? Didn't he know that Paul said, "I would that you all speak in tongues" (1 Corinthians 14:5), and doesn't that include us today? To make matters worse, the professor managed to persuade a couple of my friends that they did not really have the gift of tongues at all. I loved and respected these men, but now they had abandoned their beliefs. How could they do such a thing? How could they?

23

O for a Thousand Tongues

To top it all off, I was becoming increasingly aware of something that in my spiritual naiveté I had been ignorant of: the majority of sincere Christians throughout the history of the church had not spoken in tongues. I began to realize that the common belief has been that this gift was intended by God for the apostolic age.

Now some people could ignore all this, but I couldn't. In my confusion I prayed, "Lord show me the truth, and I'll stand by it and affirm it no matter what the consequences." And that's why I said sometimes prayer can get you into trouble—believe me, I know.

To the Law and to the Testimony 2

I would not recommend that anyone enter the ministry the way I did. To begin with, I was too young. I was without the benefit of seminary training. But besides these rather obvious disadvantages, there were other drawbacks as well. My first church, the Upper Room, was the perfect example.

To the Law and to the Testimony

Originally, the Upper Room was a Christian coffeehouse. It was housed in a senile, brick building that was mercifully bulldozed several years after our occupancy. The coffeehouse was surrounded. On the right side was a big bar called Merlin's, and on the left side was a runty grill called Shad's Red Hots. Across the street was a movie theatre and another bar, with the Illinois Central Railroad tracks running directly behind. The coffeehouse served as the strategic center of our evangelistic operations and was the ideal location for reaching the people we wanted to reach. As time passed and our numbers grew, the Upper Room coffeehouse became our church.

I have many fond memories of the Upper Room. There amid the crumbling plaster (which we painted deep purple), seated on those rough-hewn benches or on that cold brick floor, there with the crying babies and an occasional dog or two, we gathered on Sunday mornings to worship our Lord. We worshipped God and served Him with a simplicity and zeal that I have seldom seen elsewhere. Dear friends were married at the coffeehouse. But above all, many prodigals, who had wandered far from their homes and into the thralldom of sin, discovered freedom and a new life.

I have some amusing memories, too, most of which are related to my preaching. Our meetings were often crowded beyond capacity as I stood behind my first pulpit—

the coffee counter. With thirty-six varieties of tea to my left, with two steaming coffee pots to my right, and with the cream and sugar in front of me, I exhorted the brethren with many words. At strategic points throughout my sermon, the steam in one of the coffee pots would raise the lid and emit a long, lonely lament and then shut with a disapproving clank. And this was by no means the only strange thing that happened during my sermons. Frequently an insufferably long freight train would thunder past, making communication exceedingly difficult. But even more disconcerting, someone who was either drunk or on drugs would occasionally decide to join our service. And, unlike some shy Christians, these uninhibited fellows never hesitated to share their "gifts" with the body. They would spue out their uninspired commentary on whatever I happened to be preaching.

There are sad memories, too, like Jimmy Buster. I always thought there was something tragic about him; it seemed as if Jimmy was destined for misery. He was raised in the very worst kind of poverty, and at much too young an age he became an alcoholic. I think one of the things that troubled me most about Jimmy was that he was my peer.

I'm convinced that Jimmy was a gentle person at heart, but somehow he always managed to get himself into trouble. Sometimes he would wander into the

29

coffeehouse with a cut over his eye or with his nose bleeding. And what a sight he was with that gaunt body, those sunken eyes, and that cadaverous face. Usually he reeked of cheap liquor, and when he spoke it was with the pathetic eloquence of a punch-drunk boxer.

We tried to help Jimmy. We listened to his ramblings, prayed with him, encouraged him to come to church, and bought him meals. But despite our efforts we just couldn't reach him. Eventually, Jimmy died of an overdose.

In spite of my many shortcomings, as well as the general confusion that was typical of those days, there was one thing that I had going for me: at the moment of my conversion, God planted in my soul an unquenchable desire for His Word. It was like a fire burning within, and I will never forget the joy of reading the Holy Scriptures for the very first time.

I remember working my way through the New Testament, and coming to Paul's eloquent description of love in 1 Corinthians 13. It was truly sweeter than honey to my truth-starved heart. The sheer beauty and majesty of that passage made me think that if ever God had spoken, surely these were His words.

I also remember reading the twenty-third psalm for the first time. David's portrait of God as his shepherd seemed thoroughly lovely. I felt quite deprived, never having learned the psalm as a child. And so, I committed it to memory, thinking it would be a source of great comfort and strength. What a tragedy it would be, I thought, to go through life without those words hidden in my heart.

Often I heard Christians testify of various spiritual experiences. They spoke of visions, of rapturous prayer, and of feeling the power of God bodily. Although I envied these fortunate brethren, experiences of this nature were never mine. However, there was one dimension of Christian living that afforded me deep satisfaction: as the disciples' hearts burned within them when Christ opened the Scriptures on the road to Emmaus, so my most memorable and uplifting spiritual experiences were those hours when Christ opened His Word to me. Often in the first years of my ministry I knelt and prayed Psalm 119 in its entirety. The psalmist's love for God's Word seemed to perfectly express the desires of my own heart: "For I delight in your commandments because I love them. I reach out my hands for your commandments, which I love, and I meditate on your decrees" (Psalm 119:47-48).

Now it was because of this love for God's Word that I was quite willing to surrender any conviction or experience of mine that seemed contrary to it. Indeed, after I was saved, I abandoned my former beliefs with enthusiasm. To me, all the wisdom of this world could not compare with the simple truths of Scripture. So when my belief in the gift of tongues was challenged, I approached this problem with that same attitude. I decided to examine the arguments of those who insisted that the gift of tongues had ceased after the apostolic age. I was confident that if my gift were genuine, it would stand up to critical examination. "To the law and to the testimony! If they do not speak according to this word, they have no light of dawn" (Isaiah 8:20).

I began by collecting all the books I could find against speaking in tongues. There were many, and as I read them I categorized the various kinds of arguments that were supposed to prove that present day tongues speaking is not authentic. I discovered that there were basically six kinds of arguments.

First, there were the *ad hominem* arguments, or those arguments that attacked the persons holding the beliefs rather than the beliefs themselves. These were myriad. They said charismatics were divisive. They were imbalanced. Fanatical. Immature. Exclusive. Conformist sheep following their leaders. Some even attributed speaking in tongues to the power of the devil.

Too often these arguments were unkind and sarcastic, so naturally they tended to repel me. There were too many jokes at the charismatic's expense. These jokes were usually based upon stories the authors had heard about peculiar charismatics, or they were gleaned from certain television shows. Sometimes this bordered on sheer mockery. A typical example is a story I heard repeated again and again. A seminarian or a professor would go to a charismatic meeting and pretend to give a message in tongues. He would do this by reciting a passage of the Bible in Greek or Hebrew. Then when it was falsely interpreted—as it invariably would be—he would triumphantly declare that he had proved speaking in tongues to be false. But what did this irreverent mockery prove except that the individuals who perpetrated it could take advantage of uneducated people? Carlyle said, "Sarcasm is the language of the devil." Perhaps it was the critics and not the charismatics who were speaking in Satan's tongue.

What did these authors (many of whom were preachers) think they were accomplishing with all their cynicism? They certainly were not going to persuade any charismatic this way. Besides, didn't they realize that we charismatics could play the *ad hominem* game as well? Didn't these evangelical and fundamentalist preachers realize that people who live in glass houses should not throw stones?

A second frequently encountered argument was the psychological argument. This was the idea that tongues can be explained in psychological rather than spiritual terms. In addition, proponents of the psychological argument often implied that speaking in tongues was not the most healthy activity one could engage in—mentally, that is.

Some thought that tongues could be explained as a kind of mild hypnotic trance induced by autosuggestion. Others felt that speaking in tongues was the attempt of an immature individual to regress psychologically to a sort of infantile babbling. One explanation that particularly intrigued me was that speaking in tongues was cryptomnesia. (Sounds like something out of Superman comic books, doesn't it?) Cryptomnesia, or exalted memory, is the theory that at some time in a person's life, he is exposed to one foreign language or another. Although the language is never learned, it is stored in the subconscious mind. Then, in a moment of great stress, something is triggered and the person begins to utter the language which has been recorded in his subconscious. This experience can also be induced under hypnosis.

There are several problems with this theory. First, cryptomnesia is a very rare phenomenon, but speaking in tongues is quite common. Second, cryptomnesia has to be triggered by certain psychological conditions that usually put the person in a trance-like state. But these conditions are rarely present when one is speaking in tongues (which, by the way, the charismatic can engage in at will). Finally, cryptomnesia is a disorienting experience that doesn't produce the pleasant effects of speaking in tongues.

An experience I had at a conference on pastoral counseling in Philadelphia made learning this bit of obscure information worthwhile. A few of us got into a discussion about speaking in tongues, and I, of course, was the counsel for the defense. After discussing the pros and cons, one of the other pastors spoke up.

"I can explain speaking in tongues. It's nothing more than exalted memory," he said in a knowing tone of voice.

I was delighted that he had brought that up. "You mean cryptomnesia, don't you?" I asked in an equally knowing tone of voice. I'll never forget the astonished look on his face as I proceeded to voice my objections to his theory.

Still there is one basic problem that I thought was common to all these attempts to explain speaking in tongues in psychological terms: couldn't this same technique be used to disprove *any* spiritual experience? Don't the same psychologists who account for tongues speaking in this manner resort to similar arguments to disprove conversion, regeneration, and answered prayer? "Blessed is the man who does not walk in the counsel of the wicked" (Psalm 1:1).

Third was the historical argument. For example, Joseph Dillow writes, "It is the considered judgment of the leading church historians that there has been no reoccurrence of the tongues phenomenon of the first century in succeeding centuries."[1] But I wondered, what were the presuppositions of these "leading church historians?" I could cite professors of church history who would assert just the opposite, and who, furthermore, would characterize such statements as "sweeping generalizations."[2]

Sure, it could be shown that tongues had greatly diminished, but how could it be shown that tongues had ceased altogether? This would be virtually impossible to do. Also, I could think of no reason why God in His sovereignty could not withhold the gift during certain periods of history for reasons of His own. Then, too, there was John Wesley's explanation for the cessation of spiritual gifts: "Because the love of many waxed cold. . . . this was the real cause why the extraordinary gifts of the Holy Ghost were no longer to be found in the Christian church."

A fourth kind of argument was what I called the anthropological argument. Joseph Dillow forcefully presents this argument: "Tongues speaking as manifested today is a purely heathen concept. . . . Pagan tribes all over the world have been speaking in tongues for centuries. The similarities between their practice and that of the modern tongues movement are striking. At its root the movement is simply a merger of Christianity with paganism."[3]

As I read this I wondered, is this fair? Is modern tongues speaking purely a heathen concept? Is the charismatic movement really a merger of Christianity with paganism? I thought it a shame to have to resort to this. Whether the charismatics are right or wrong, they base their beliefs upon the Bible.

Furthermore, to assert that "pagan tribes" have been speaking in tongues for centuries, and then to classify the tongues speech of charismatic Christians in the same category, is at best a gross over-simplification.

37

To the Law and to the Testimony

The linguistic argument was the fifth type. This argument may be stated as follows. The Bible teaches that genuine speaking in tongues is in the form of known languages. But linguists have proven that contemporary speaking in tongues is not in the form of known languages. Therefore, contemporary claims to possess the gift of tongues are false.

Of all the arguments that I found against speaking in tongues, this was the one I considered to be most convincing. Perhaps some charismatics could dismiss it by saying that speaking in tongues is the language of angels,[4] and therefore is not susceptible to linguistic analysis. But for my part, I could not accept this explanation. In my view, when Paul spoke of the tongues of angels, he was simply using hyperbole to emphasize his point. Furthermore, on the day of Pentecost (Acts 2), tongues are portrayed as being actual languages understood by those who heard. Therefore, I was willing to admit that if my gift was truly Pentecostal, that is, if it was the same kind of phenomenon that occurred on the day of Pentecost, then it should be in the form of an actual language.

I dealt with the linguistic argument in two ways. First, I minimized the appropriateness of trying to resolve this issue via linguistic analysis. To subject recorded samples of tongues to linguistic analysis, to my mind at least, seemed to be irreverent. This seemed akin to trying to locate God with a telescope. There were other problems, too. For example, no two linguists would ever transcribe the same recorded sample of tongues speech in the same way.[5] Then of course, since most sincere Christians would not submit to having their spiritual gifts dissected in a laboratory, how could the linguist obtain any kind of sample that would be truly representative?

Second, I simply accepted by faith that my tongues speaking was an actual language. What may sound like a series of grunts and incoherent mutterings to an untrained ear may in fact be an actual language. Perhaps some Christians were muttering gibberish, but did this prove that I was? Then again, perhaps there were times when my own speaking in tongues degenerated into fleshly gibberish, but did this prove that *all* of my tongues speech was gibberish? I decided that I would regard my gift as being genuine until proven (in the strongest sense of the word) to be false. Innocent until proven guilty.

The sixth and final argument was the biblical argument. This, of course, was the attempt to use various passages of Scripture to prove that tongues were for the apostolic age only. If the linguistic argument seemed most threatening, I must say that the biblical argument seemed least threatening. It was apparent to me that anyone reading the New Testament for the first time would presume that the exercise of spiritual gifts was a normal part of church life.

One thing that impressed me unfavorably about how the biblical argument was presented was that some of the authors seemed to have woefully inadequate conceptions of precisely what speaking in tongues is, and how it is used. First Corinthians, chapters twelve through fourteen, were positively tortured by some commentators. For example, some asserted that when Paul said, "I thank God that I speak in tongues more than all of you" (1 Corinthians 14:18), he was referring to his natural talent for speaking foreign languages. As if the whole chapter were about the use and abuse of foreign languages in the church!

It was also asserted that the gift of tongues was used in the New Testament exclusively for preaching the gospel, and that charismatic claims to pray in tongues were therefore erroneous. But the truth is that all manifestations of the gift of tongues are in the form of speech. Anything that can be done through the medium of ordinary speech can also be done through the extraordinary speech of tongues. Paul plainly tells us that the early Christians could speak in tongues, pray in tongues, sing in tongues, bless in tongues, and give thanks in tongues (1 Corinthians 14:14-17). Be-

40

sides, the entire context of 1 Corinthians 14 is not that of evangelistic proclamation, but of the gathering of the church for mutual edification.[6]

Although some good points were made in these books, on the whole their biblical arguments were unsatisfactory to me. There were just too many gaps. Too often, instead of presenting the facts in the light of the Scriptures taken as a whole, proof texts were cited that didn't seem to prove anything. For example, it was frequently asserted that these spiritual gifts were not for today because the canon of Scripture is closed. This is an important and compelling argument. However, instead of citing the broad evidence that proves this to be the case, the authors would present a dubious interpretation of 1 Corinthians 13:2-13: since the perfect has come, tongues have ceased. But the vast majority of commentators agreed that *the perfect* does not refer to the closing of the canon. Thus, a valid criticism was weakened by the questionable interpretation of a text.

After prayerfully examining these various arguments against speaking in tongues, my faith in the gift was still intact. I went to the law and the testimony, and at that time I found that the light of the critics was less than overwhelming. I was more determined than ever to hold my belief in speaking in tongues. So I gathered my notes together, assembled the various arguments, and set out to disprove them "line upon line, precept upon precept." I preached a series of sermons entitled *Tongues: A Biblical Defense*, and I felt that I dealt quite adequately with the objections that had been raised.

Even though my belief in tongues emerged basically unscathed from this time of testing, I did feel there were many important concerns and objections expressed about the charismatic movement. There *was* theological immaturity. But didn't they realize they were throwing out the baby with the bathwater? Charismatics are guilty of certain excesses and imbalances, but this is not grounds for rejecting the charismatic movement part and parcel.

The solution to this problem was correction not rejection. So, I determined to shun the imbalanced extremes of the charismatic movement. I would try to prove by my life that spiritual gifts could flourish and edify the church in a healthy, sane atmosphere. My task was clear: live the balanced charismatic life. However, this was not going to be as simple as I thought.

To the Law and to the Testimony

NOTES

[1] Joseph Dillow, *Speaking in Tongues: Seven Crucial Questions*, (Grand Rapids, Michigan: Zondervan Publishing House, 1975), p. 153.

[2] E. Glenn Hinson, "The Significance of Glossolalia in the History of Christianity," *Speaking in Tongues: Let's Talk About It*, ed. Watson E. Mills (Waco, Texas: Word Books, 1973), p. 63.

[3] Dillow, p. 189.

[4] 1 Corinthians 13:1.

[5] William J. Samarin, "Glossolalia as a Vocal Phenomenon, " *Speaking in Tongues: Let's Talk About It*, ed. Watson E. Mills (Waco, Texas: Word Books, 1973), p.132. Samarin states:

In the absence of clues given by meaning, a person transcribing a glossic text is left to subtle, phonological cues, and his segmentation of the whole sound continuum into small units will be guided in considerable part by the prejudices that he brings to the task. A single text will likely have as many different transcriptions as there are people to attempt the task.

[6] Of course, 1 Corinthians 14:23 does speak of ungifted and unbelieving people entering the worship service. In that case, special instructions are in order. Still, the chapter deals primarily with the church gathering for mutual edification.

The Burden of the Prophets 3

It wasn't speaking in tongues that made my efforts to live the balanced charismatic life so difficult; it was the gift of prophecy. As I have said, speaking in tongues was pleasurable enough. But to prophesy—to declare the burden of the Lord as the prophets themselves described the experience[1]—well, that is another story altogether.

The Burden of the Prophets

Prophetic messages were quite common at our church. In fact, whenever we assembled to worship, spiritual gifts, especially the gift of prophecy, were foremost in our minds. Even though we followed no prescribed liturgy, there was an unwritten order of worship that always included the opportunity for one to prophesy according to the proportion of his faith (Romans 12:6). And everyone was urged to participate: "What then shall we say, brothers? When you come together, everyone has a hymn, or a word of instruction, a revelation, a tongue or an interpretation" (1 Corinthians 14:26).

Our worship service usually began with singing. Our songs were primarily Scripture set to music, and we sang them with or without accompaniment. We stood. We clapped. We sang with all our hearts to the Lord. After a song ended, it was often followed by a spontaneous burst of applause. Hands, like flags proudly waving, stretched toward heaven amid shouts of joy. "Oh clap your hands, all ye people; shout unto God with the voice of triumph" (Psalm 47:1 KJV). The crescendo of praise would peak in a moment of dramatic silence. Then we would wait upon the Lord, every heart expectant, every mind wondering. Finally, some brave soul would prophesy:

> Let not your heart be troubled or
> fearful. For in My Father's house
> are many mansions. When I come

46

again, I will come and take you to
myself. Do not be discouraged,
but make steady paths for your
feet. Walk straight. I would have
you gaze intently upon Me. Do
not be discouraged or down-
hearted because I am coming
again to bring you to Myself and
you shall never be apart from Me.[2]

Our prophecies seldom if ever pre-
dicted the future. Instead they took the form
of fervent exhortations or simple words of
comfort. Generally they consisted of various
biblical phrases and fragments pieced together like a patchwork quilt. Often they focused upon such themes as the imminent
return of Christ or God's forgiving love. Most
of the time the prophecies were spoken in
the first person as if God Himself were ad-
dressing us, but occasionally the phrase
thus saith the Lord was used even as it was
by the prophets of the Bible.

Sometimes prophecies were judged
to be spurious. These prophecies contained
a statement or sentiment that was clearly
contrary to Scripture. We did not regard
these prophecies as deliberately deceptive,
but rather as the overzealous attempts of
some misguided saint. In such cases the elders, after conferring together, would advise
the congregation to disregard that message.
The person who spoke it was urged not to be
discouraged, but to be more cautious in the

future. I remember one prophecy that I considered particularly "creative." A visitor amazed us all by imperiously speaking the following prophecy in a pronounced Brooklyn accent: "For behold—I the Lord Thy God—am ionic. I am crackling with energy!" The problem with this prophecy was that it was not clear whether the prophet was referring to the God of the Bible or a toasted breakfast cereal! However, prophecies were seldom judged to be spurious. For the most part, they were welcomed as messages of "edification and exhortation and consolation" (1 Corinthians 14:3 NASB).

When it came to spiritual gifts, I was not content to be a mere spectator. I was determined that if God were willing, I too would prophesy. After all, didn't Paul say ". . . eagerly desire spiritual gifts, especially the gift of prophecy" (1 Corinthians 14:1)? So I did.

"Just what is it like to prophesy?" I asked a friend.

"That's simple," he assured me. "Prophesying is like interpreting a message in tongues only there are no tongues." Then, noting my evident dissatisfaction with his explanation, he clarified it: "You know, like speaking in tongues—only in English." What my friend was trying to say was that prophecy, like speaking in tongues, is a supernatural utterance given by the Holy

The Burden of the Prophets

Spirit; but unlike tongues, prophecy is given in the native language of the speaker. So, armed with that definition, I proceeded in my ongoing quest for spiritual gifts.

My first attempt to prophesy was similar to jumping off the high dive for the first time: I did it with much fear and trembling. In fact, it was downright traumatic. You see, it is all very well and good to be eager to prophesy. But when a word actually comes to you—at an actual meeting—in front of actual people—there are several obstacles that must be hurdled. These obstacles loom before your mind, daring you to advance. To appreciate this, imagine you are at a meeting. You believe that the Spirit of the Lord is stirring your spirit, and you feel He wants you to prophesy. Here's what might happen.

First, there would be dread, because the very thought of prophesying is inherently awesome. After all, who are you to presume to speak on behalf of "the high and lofty One that inhabiteth eternity, whose name is Holy" (Isaiah 57:15 KJV)? Shall dust speak on behalf of the Almighty?

Second, there would be more dread as you contemplate answering for your words on the day of judgment. If men shall account for every idle word they speak (Matthew 12:36), how much more shall they account for those words spoken in the very name of the Lord of Hosts? You hope that

The Burden of the Prophets

when you stand before Him on that day and say, "Lord, Lord, did we not prophesy in your name?" His answer will not be, "I never knew you. Away from me, you evildoers" (Matthew 7:22, 23).

Third, what if you fail? If you begin to prophesy, who's to say you will be able to finish? You might start off well enough, but then falter and that would be the end of it. Like Peter, you might impetuously venture forth upon the waves, but then, when you actually realized where you were . . .

Fourth, there is always the possibility that your prophecy might turn out to be something less than inspirational. Not that it would be false, mind you. It's just that new wine can go flat. Instead of being acclaimed by the chorus of hallelujahs and amens you expected, your prophecy would be followed by an embarrassing silence, with the exception of a few people clearing their throats perhaps.

Fifth, and worst of all, what if you give a false prophecy? It might be that you were speaking purely from the flesh, or you could even have been led astray by darker forces. Your mind is filled with visions of the elders saying, "Don't be discouraged, Brother," as you collapse on the floor like Ananias and Sapphira, never to rise again.

Finally, if because of these concerns

The Burden of the Prophets

you do not prophesy, then in that case, you have quenched the Holy Spirit. So you go home feeling miserable and guilty, knowing that the opportunity is gone forever. And you wonder, now that you have buried your one talent, will God give it to someone else with ten?

However, if you successfully overcome these obstacles, you are ready to prophesy. But how do you know when to do it? Well, if you are an observer of the signs of the times, you'll know. For when prophetic pressure mounts within your soul, there are certain tell-tale signs that indicate a prophecy is about to be born. These signs are varied, and of course everyone has their own idiosyncrasies. But generally speaking, you can expect your prophetic message to be preceded by such phenomena as a rapid pulse, sweaty palms, labored breathing, blushing or turning pale, and a diverse mixture of chills and tingling sensations. But finally, duty impatiently whispers its ultimatum in your ear: Now or never!—so you speak.

Now undoubtedly, as you grow more adept at prophesying, the trauma associated with it will subside considerably. And there will be a growing sense of satisfaction. Namely, the incomparable honor of speaking on behalf of God. But nevertheless, such are the burdens of the prophets.

The Burden of the Prophets

In spite of these burdens, I have to admit there was something distinctly romantic about the notion of prophesying. There you are standing in succession to the prophets of the Bible. Samuel and Elijah saw your day coming and were glad. True, your lips are unclean, but they have been touched by a live coal from off the altar. Like Isaiah, you have heard the voice of the Lord saying. "Whom shall I send, and who will go for us?" And you responded, "Here am I. Send me!"

And the people around you—just what did they expect to see: A reed shaking in the wind? A man dressed in soft clothing? No! They want a prophet; someone who will stand before the Herods and the Pilates and the Caiaphases and boldly proclaim the word of the Lord. They want a man with a message, an uncompromising *thus saith the Lord* for a crooked and perverse generation.

Yes, it was all very romantic. But gradually, what had started as a romantic venture, an idealistic quest for spiritual gifts, was slowly, imperceptibly changing. Into what, I wasn't sure. All I knew was that the excitement and romance of prophesying was turning into an uneasy sense that the prophecies I heard, including my own, were hardly worthy of the name. The idea that they were the words of the living God was beginning to seem painfully ludicrous. Would

The Burden of the Prophets

the romance now become a comedy of errors, or a tragedy, perhaps? At any rate, one thing was certain: this burden of the prophets was becoming a crushing, onerous weight. And I couldn't help wondering if the weight which I was carrying was not the burden of the Lord at all, but some foreign yoke of bondage.

How do I account for this transformation? With great difficulty, for change is such a mysterious process. This is especially true when it takes the form of denying a strong belief or renouncing a cherished experience. Such change rarely occurs by passing successively through certain logical steps. Rather there is a complex of factors involved, spiritual as well as psychological, mental as well as emotional, which all play a part in leading a soul to that moment when a new conviction is born.

In my case, there were four simple words that played a decisive role in changing my heart: thus saith the Lord. To me, these were most unsettling words. And the more I comprehended their meaning, the more I understood what the prophets meant when they spoke them and what the Holy Spirit meant when He inspired them, the more unsettling they became.

Thus saith the Lord. It is a rich, a pregnant phrase. When a prophet said "thus saith the Lord," he meant that the very word of God was being proclaimed, and that as such it was invested with divine authority. These words also convey the ideas of infallibility and purity—for could God's word be anything less? And as this phrase became ever brighter and more powerful to me, the prophecies that I had spoken and heard others speak paled and diminished to the point of nothingness. I could not help but think that if the prophecies spoken in our church were actually related to the prophecies recorded in Scripture, then they were distant relatives indeed.

Thus saith the Lord. At first I thought that I could avoid those words. Perhaps I could disassociate them from my prophecies altogether. Yes, I would continue to prophesy, but I would not let those dread words pass through my lips again. There would be no "thus saith the Lord" from this prophet. I could no longer make any such claim. I believed that my prophecies were blessed by the Holy Spirit, but they were not inspired. And so I tried to salve my conscience by assuming that contemporary prophecies were characterized by a sort of mid-range inspiration: higher than a good sermon but lower than the Scriptures.

My problem, however, could hardly be solved by simply refraining from speaking the phrase "thus saith the Lord" when I prophesied, or by positing a kind of mid-range inspiration for which I could find no support in the Scriptures. For the very phrase and the meaning it conveys are woven into the whole concept of prophecy. You can't disassociate "thus saith the Lord" from prophecy. Whether or not one speaks the actual phrase when one prophesies is not the point. The truth is that the very act of prophesying speaks a loud and clear "thus saith the Lord" whether the actual words are uttered or not.

Thus saith the Lord. When the prophets in the Bible spoke those words, they were based upon definite revelations that were granted to them by God. In Old Testament times prophets were called seers because of the visions they beheld. But what evidence was there that any of our prophecies had their origin in a revelation given by God's Spirit? Ezekiel protested, "This is what the Sovereign LORD says: Woe to the foolish prophets who follow their own spirit and have seen nothing!" (Ezekiel 13:3). In the final analysis, isn't that what we were—prophets who had seen nothing? What evidence was there that we were not just following our own spirits instead of the Spirit of God? I could find no evidence in the Bible that prophecies were communicated by mere intuition or subjective impressions. And yet, in nearly all cases this is how ours were received. And these impressions and intuitions could not be authenticated in any kind of objective sense.

The Burden of the Prophets

Thus saith the Lord. In the Bible, when a man was commissioned to speak those words, God confirmed them in an extraordinary manner. God's prophets were given predictions that were fulfilled in amazing ways. In addition to this, God confirmed their words with mighty signs and wonders.

Paul describes a typical response to the gift of prophecy in the New Testament church as follows. "But if an unbeliever or someone who does not understand comes in while everybody is prophesying, he will be convinced by all that he is a sinner and will be judged by all, and the secrets of his heart will be laid bare. So he will fall down and worship God, exclaiming, 'God is really among you!'" (1 Corinthians 14:24,25). But where are such phenomena to be found today? Where are the prophecies whose content displays a power that trancends merely human ability? How I longed to hear somebody cry out under pain of conviction that the secrets of his heart had been revealed, or that God was in our midst. But such things just didn't happen—the razor sharpness of God's two-edged sword was not evident.

Claims to such miraculous phenomena abound, but factual evidence is scarce. A full discussion would fill books, but I can only say here that I heard and read literally hundreds of such claims while I was a charismatic pastor; I attended healing meetings both large and small, famous and un-

The Burden of the Prophets

known. I have spoken to dozens of people who have claimed to experience the kinds of signs and wonders that are spoken of in the book of Acts. I tried very hard to believe these claims. I tried to separate the wheat from the chaff, and to allow charitably for mistakes of human frailty. I do believe that God is a supernatural God who answers prayers and intervenes in our lives in exciting and miraculous ways. Nevertheless, my conclusion in this matter is that contemporary claims to fulfilled prophetic predictions and works of power are scarcely worthy to be compared with those miracles recorded on the pages of Scripture.

Thus saith the Lord. What abuses I had seen of those words. What bitter fruit I had seen borne by men and women speaking those words. I have seen people married on the basis of guidance received from personal prophecies only to be divorced a week later because of a terrible scandal. Many lives have been harmed by such prophetic guidance. What actions, what conduct, have been countenanced by a "thus saith the Lord." Also, I was ashamed that on many occasions I had failed to preserve the sanctity of those words. There were times when I heard that phrase appended to an utterance that I knew in my heart was unworthy of it. Yet I, a pastor, chose to remain silent. I chose to ignore the truth which was becoming so apparent.

57

The Burden of the Prophets

If only I had been content to speak in tongues. I could speak in tongues quite innocently because there was no "thus saith the Lord." As Paul said, "For anyone who speaks in a tongue does not speak to men, but to God. Indeed, no one understands him; he utters mysteries with his spirit." (1 Corinthians 14:2). I longed to drown my doubts in those mysteries that no one understands. For as long as I did not understand what I was speaking, my mind could be at ease. God understood. But the trouble was that I was beginning to understand prophecy. In fact, I understood it too well, for the curtain was drawn back and the mystery vanished. No longer could I take refuge in the unknown.

Thus saith the Lord. How I struggled with those words! As Jacob wrestled with the angel in the dark of the night, so I wrestled with those words. As the angel wounded Jacob, so those words wounded me. And as Jacob's defeat became his victory, I thank God those words—so right and unfathomable in their significance—defeated me.

The moment of truth came when I heard a prophecy spoken at a charismatic church I was visiting. I was sitting in the church trying to worship God while dreading the approach of that obligatory moment of silence which signaled that a prophecy was about to be spoken. The silence came,

The Burden of the Prophets

and soon it was broken by a bold and commanding "thus saith the Lord!"

Those words triggered an immediate reaction. Conviction, like water rising against a dam, began to fill my soul. "Listen my people . . ." Until finally, the dam burst: "This is not my God," I cried within my heart. "This is not my Lord!"

As Bunyan's Pilgrim was freed of his burden at the foot of the cross, so at that moment, I was freed of mine: I would never prophesy again. Now there would be no more rationalizing. No more closing my eyes. The burden of the prophets was gone forever.

NOTES

[1] See Isaiah 15:1; 17:1; 19:1; Habakkuk 1:1; Nahum 1:1; et al.

[2] This is an actual prophecy that was spoken at one of our meetings.

Truth in the Inward Parts 4

It was a great relief to shed that "prophetic burden" which had grown so intolerably heavy. I was about to discover that a new perception of truth can be as disturbing as it is liberating. This was nothing less than a spiritual upheaval—an upheaval that was bound to have repercussions not only for me personally, but for my church as well. To borrow a phrase from Paul, there were "conflicts without, fears within."

Truth in the Inward Parts

The first battle to be fought was with the fears within. These fears enter the soul in many forms. Forebodings threaten the future. Doubts erode confidence. Dogged questions clamor for answers. To contend with such internal adversaries is to come to grips with the truth "in the inward parts."

One question demanding an answer was, "Have I sinned?" This question focused with particular intensity upon my past involvement with the gift of prophecy. Since my prophecies did not originate with the Spirit of God, was I a false prophet? At first this was a conclusion that was difficult to resist! But I rejected the notion upon further reflection. Despite the fact that my prophecies were misguided, I never prophesied anything contrary to Scripture, and my motives were to glorify Christ. Furthermore, it is possible that many of my prophecies were genuine exhortations (Romans 12:8) that were misappropriated and spoken in the form of prophecies.

Yet I could not help feeling that there was more than just error involved in all of this. Because to dare to prophesy, to invoke the authority of Almighty God for a merely human utterance, betrays more than simple ignorance or misguided zeal. It betrays an ignorance which is culpable because it is rooted in spiritual pride. So I owned my actions for what they were—unexcused sin.

Truth in the Inward Parts

Consequently, guilt, with all its breakers, rolled over my soul. There was regret—regret that I had ever prophesied; regret that will remain with me as long as I live. There was humiliation—like that of a foolish child. There was shame—for my incredible presumption. But finally, there was peace, for "there is forgiveness with Thee, that Thou mayest be feared" (Psalm 130:4 KJV).

But it wasn't just the aftermath of my prophecies that had to be dealt with; there was also the gift of tongues. Could it be that tongues, like prophecy, would also have to be abandoned? Since a message in tongues is functionally equivalent to a prophecy, this seemed likely. Therefore, another question demanding an answer was, "Do I really have the gift of tongues?"

In the past I had concluded that the linguistic argument was the most potent critique of contemporary tongues speech. Even then, I think I realized (in my heart at least) that my tongues were not a linguistically definable language. And now the argument came to me with renewed force. No one could listen to me speaking in tongues and then marvel that the mighty acts of God were being proclaimed in an understandable language. And so this fact alone was enough to invalidate the gift for me.

I suppose that I could have sidestepped this line of reasoning by taking

63

refuge in the idea that tongues are not necessarily a known language. But even so, I still had to admit that the Scriptures teach that tongues are a miraculous gift. What happened on the day of Pentecost was a miracle! Luke describes the gift of tongues as an utterance given by the Holy Spirit (Acts 2:4). Paul speaks of tongues as a sign (1 Corinthians 14:22). Therefore, even if tongues aren't necessarily a known language, I still had to ask myself, "Is there any evidence that my tongues speech is of a miraculous nature? Is there any indication that my utterances originated with the Holy Spirit and not just my own mind?"

I had to be completely honest with myself about this, because it is so easy to rationalize an experience in which one has invested a great deal of spiritual and emotional energy. It is extremely difficult to be objective about experiences we think have brought us closer to Jesus and made us intimate with the Holy Spirit. On the one hand, I feared to quench the Holy Spirit, and so dishonor the Giver by questioning His gift. But, on the other hand, I feared self-deception and error. In such circumstances one can only pray, "O God, be tender in your judgments."

Finally, I admitted it to myself. The truth is there was nothing miraculous about this "gift" of mine—I *learned* to speak in tongues. Here was no sign to marvel at. I had attained fluency in my tongues speech through practice, not by the sudden power of the Holy Spirit. And in retrospect, I can see I was guided more by the peer pressure of my well-meaning friends than by the Holy Spirit.

Nevertheless, I must confess that at first I didn't want to stop speaking in tongues. I had grown so accustomed to the practice that the prospect of quitting was like parting company with an old friend. Quitting was especially distasteful because speaking in tongues had seemed to be such an enriching aspect of my personal devotions. To stop now, after all those years, left a spiritual vacuum in my devotional life that my soul abhorred.

However, I soon began to realize that speaking in tongues was not as edifying as I had previously thought. How could it be, since I was uttering words and phrases of my own invention? Therefore, I was beginning to understand that, far from being a deeper dimension of prayer, praying in tongues was an evasion—a failure to grapple with the profundities of prayer.

I have always felt there is an aura of mystery surrounding prayer. At no time are we more aware of our weakness and inadequacy than when we kneel to pray. As Paul said, "we do not know how to pray as we should" (Romans 8:26 NASB). In the face of such spiritual helplessness, tongues can become a crutch. For example, when I found myself mute and dumb in His presence, I could far too quickly remedy the situation by praying in tongues. Again, when I was oppressed with a sense of guilt and felt alienated from God, it was far more easy to pray in tongues than to search my heart for the cause of the guilt. But what was all of this if it was not an evasion? Whereas previously I could avoid the difficulties inherent in prayer by resorting to tongues, now I found myself praying, "Lord, teach me to pray."

Undoubtedly, the most profound prayer is one which, having faced obstacles and hindrances by faith, fights its way through to the throne of grace. The need is not for a "prayer language," but for a truer grasp of the language of prayer. Indeed, prayer is a pouring out of the heart before God. But it reaches its more profound dimensions when it is prayed with the intensity of a Hannah, or the passion of the psalmist who wrote, "Out of the depths, O God, I cry unto Thee."

Now the time had come for me to squarely face the problem that God's people have always faced in their efforts to pray: how to express the inexpressible. In the words of the familiar hymn, "What language shall I borrow to thank Thee, dearest friend?" Precisely! What language *could* I borrow?

Truth in the Inward Parts

And so, just as I formerly had abandoned the "gift of prophecy," now I laid aside the "gift of tongues." It wasn't as if I had set out to disprove the authenticity of speaking in tongues. On the contrary! I advocated speaking in tongues. Still more, I loved speaking in tongues. And in the face of mounting evidence which contradicted the validity of my own experiences, I did everything in my power to hold fast. I searched the Scriptures. I prayed. I practiced these gifts more than many. But eventually, the gap between my experience of these gifts and their portrayal in Scripture stretched my sense of integrity to the limits.

Therefore, for me, the renunciation of these gifts was hardly an act of unbelief; rather it was an act that required no small degree of faith. It was not doubt in God's Word that led me to renounce these gifts. It was faith in the truthfulness of God's Word that led me to doubt and finally to renounce my own experiences.

Needless to say, my entire outlook on spiritual gifts was transformed as a result. I was beginning to understand that certain gifts of the Holy Spirit had a unique function in the purposes of God. In the case of tongues and prophecy, this function was twofold. First, both of these gifts were designed by God to be vehicles of verbal revelation; that is, they conveyed the Word of the Lord in human speech, by the power of the

Truth in the Inward Parts

Holy Spirit. Both of these gifts, then, are distinguished from proclamation and teaching in that they are utterances of the Spirit spoken in and through the human personality.

Thus the role of the prophets and apostles in the New Testament was to reveal the mystery of Christ. It was to them the Holy Spirit revealed that mystery which had been hidden from previous generations (Ephesians 3:3-5). It was the revelation of this mystery that made the apostles and prophets the foundation of the universal church, with Christ Himself as the cornerstone (Ephesians 2:19-21).

The second function of tongues and prophecy was to confirm and authenticate the revelations they conveyed by their miraculous character. In the case of prophecy, predictions (such as those of Agabus) and words of hidden knowledge (such as those of Elijah and Elisha) confirmed that God indeed was speaking through His prophet. In the case of tongues, the message was spoken in a language not understood by the speaker but known by those who heard (see Acts 2), likewise confirming that the speaker's utterance was of divine origin.

Thus the presence of such gifts as tongues in the church, which were generally mediated through the apostles and prophets themselves, bore startling testimony that God was unveiling a new message. Just as the miraculous works of Christ testified He was sent from God (John 5:36), so also the signs of the apostles testified they too were sent from God. "How shall we escape if we ignore such a great salvation? This salvation, which was first announced by the Lord, was confirmed to us by those who heard him. God also testified to it by signs, wonders and various miracles, and gifts of the Holy Spirit distributed according to his will" (Hebrews 2:3, 4).

The function of these gifts was fulfilled after God's revelation of Himself and of the way of salvation was gloriously consummated in Christ. Christ came, the mystery was revealed, and finally it was confirmed and recorded in those books which we call the New Testament. So then, what can present day manifestations of tongues and prophecy add to the mystery of Christ? Nothing! The inescapable dilemma is this: if the mystery of Christ has been fully revealed, then prophetic revelations can add nothing to it. If, however, tongues and prophecy are confined to the boundaries of canonical Scripture (as many assert), then they are not, properly speaking, revelations—they are repetitions and as such are superfluous. Furthermore, since these gifts functioned to confirm the giving of new revelation, then their purpose has been entirely fulfilled.

Truth in the Inward Parts

This is not to say that revelation as such has ceased. Such an assertion is grossly mistaken, because God's self-revelation never ceases. The very existence of His handiwork continually proclaims the reality of the Creator. God makes His presence evident within us (Romans 1:19), and today as always the hallmark of the children of God is that they are being led by His Spirit (Romans 8:14). Paul's prayer in Ephesians 1:17, moreover, is as relevant today as it ever was: "I keep asking that the God of our Lord Jesus Christ, the glorious Father, may give you the Spirit of wisdom and revelation, so that you may know him better." Paul was not praying that any new revelation be given to the Ephesians. He was praying that their eyes might be enlightened so as to fully appreciate the glory of that which had already been revealed. Therefore, the revelation that we need today is derived from and based upon that which has been spoken by the prophets and apostles of both testaments. This is not a revelation to those who speak, but to us who hear, that our eyes may be enlightened to apprehend the glory of God in the face of Jesus Christ.

Thus for me, the renunciation of tongues and prophecy did not represent a flight to a religion of the letter only. It did not represent a denial of the fact that our God is living and true, that ours is a God of great surprises who intervenes in history in marvelous ways and answers prayers beyond all that we can ask or think. Neither did it represent a denial of the fact that God in His sovereign pleasure is free to speak to whomever He pleases in whatever fashion, for there is an intimate communion between God and His people. What it did represent was a recognition that certain gifts of the Holy Spirit are so closely knit together with the giving of special revelation, that when that revelation reached its climax at the coming of Christ, the purpose of these gifts was fulfilled. For "God spoke to our forefathers through the prophets at many times and in various ways, but in these last days he has spoken to us by His Son . . ." (Hebrews 1:1).

The final question to be reckoned with was related to the edification value of these gifts. After all, Paul did write that "everyone who prophesies speaks to men for their strengthening, encouragement and comfort" (1 Corinthians 14:3). Would I by renouncing these gifts be forfeiting an important source of edification both for myself and the church?

To answer this question I needed only to consider what it was about these gifts that made them edifying to begin with. Was it their miraculous nature? Surely not. You don't have to delve too deeply into the New Testament before you discover that Jesus didn't exactly encourage people to seek after signs and wonders! The value of these gifts consisted not in their form—that is, their miraculous nature—but in their content. The gifts of prophecy and tongues edified the church because they conveyed inspired revelations, the substance of which has been preserved for us in the Scriptures.

What must be remembered is that for the Corinthians, the Scriptures were not sufficient. Why? Because at that time they were not complete. A Christian in first century Corinth may have had access to several letters and perhaps some oral traditions, but that was not sufficient for a full understanding of the Christian life. And so God gave to the church an abundant supply of such gifts as tongues and prophecy to convey to His people an adequate understanding of the Way. The point is that today, unlike the Corinthians, we have the completed Scriptures, and therefore there is no need for such supplementation. And these sacred writings, which are called the oracles of God, are a sufficient guide for the life of faith.

Therefore, if today we seek those gifts whose function was to convey special revelation, we are in actuality not progressing, but regressing. What are these gifts but the vehicles, mere vessels, of those revelations that are now contained in our Bibles? How then can we advance spiritually by focusing upon those gifts whose function was to convey the revelations which we have already received? So the need is not for revelatory gifts. Rather, the need is for greater enlightenment, greater interpretation, and a greater application of that which we already possess.

Formerly I studied this issue and had concluded that tongues and prophecy should be practiced in the church today. Now with eight years of experience under my belt—experience which I am convinced is typical of the charismatic movement as a whole—I have reversed my position. It wasn't that I discovered any new doctrines. It was just a better application of truths which I had already believed. My beliefs may have evolved doctrinally, but in the final analysis, it was integrity, not theology, that led me to abandon these gifts.

Go Tell It to Your Brethren 5

In view of my recent changes, my life would have been considerably less complicated had I not been pastoring a charismatic church at that time. However, I was. And so, what do you do? What do you do when you've pastored a charismatic church for eight years, when you've spoken in tongues daily for nine or ten years, when you've prophesied, thinking all the while that you

Go Tell It to Your Brethren

were proclaiming the Word of the Lord, when you've prayed for others and have helped them to receive these same experiences, when you've taught about these gifts again and again; and not only that, when you've defended them publicly and vowed you'd never change, only to find that your convictions have changed in spite of it all? What do you do?

You ask, seek, and knock. You weigh alternatives. You procrastinate as much as you dare. You scrutinize your motives, conscious all the while that only God truly knows the secrets of the heart. One thing was certain: I couldn't go on leading charismatic worship services as if nothing had changed. So that left just two alternatives: I could resign my pastorate, or I could share my new beliefs with the church in the hope that others might come to see the merits of my position.

There were weighty reasons for resigning. In the first place, the church was charismatic; virtually the entire congregation spoke in tongues and a good number prophesied. I knew that if I took my case to the church it would be shaken to its very foundations. Several things could happen as a result of this. The church could collapse altogether and disband. Perhaps worse, it could split into factions. And even if my position should prevail, we were bound to lose members. Undoubtedly, the church would enter a period of great testing—greater than any we had ever faced before.

Nevertheless, there were other considerations. I was one of the founders of the church, and from the beginning, my teaching had informed the church's theological stance. Furthermore, although our church was charismatic by practice, we had no creedal commitment to charismatic doctrines. Our church was still in the process of evolving, both theologically and otherwise. Therefore, I would be violating no vows or creeds by seeking to change the church's position through due process.

It wasn't that I had become bitter or felt compelled to thrust my opinions upon others. I did not relish the prospect of inaugurating a controversy. The great preacher Phillips Brooks said in one of his sermons, "The man who thinks to make much of the fuller truth to which he has come, by upbraiding the partial truth by which he has come to it, is a poor creature." I had no desire to become that poor creature.

Neither did I desire to repudiate the charismatic movement as a whole. I believe that the charismatic movement, though flawed in some respects, is of God. Many people, myself included, owe their eternal salvation to the evangelistic fervor of the charismatics, and I recognized there was much to be salvaged from my charismatic past. In the early seventies, when I and other young people were discovering the reality of Jesus Christ, many of the institutional churches spurned us because of our life-styles; yet humble charismatic saints were eager to extend to us the right hand of fellowship. They taught us that the Christian life is joyous. They worshiped God in a manner that seemed to approximate the ideals of worship exhibited in the Psalms. And they emphasized that the church is more than an institution; it is a body made up of many members, all of whom, whether small or great, have been endowed by God with gifts and ministries.

However, at the same time, there is a dark side of the charismatic movement—a side I have chosen not to focus upon in this book. Too often, beneath the smiles and up-lifted hands lurk emptiness and repressed fears. Spiritual pride and theological aberration are not uncommon. There are the casualties and shipwrecks, too. The newspapers keep us well informed of misguided people who, by abandoning medical knowledge, have suffered self-inflicted tragedy. And I have seen fanaticism so extreme that some have been driven to desperation and even insanity. These characteristics are by no means typical of all charismatics. Nevertheless, as truth liberates, error inevitably leads to bondage. As a pastor, I longed to see the people whom God had entrusted to my oversight protected from such bondage. Thus, it was because of the dark side of the charismatic movement that I chose to present my case to the church. And if my testimony should lead to my dismissal from the church . . . so be it.

The first mistake I made was in sharing my new convictions with my closest friends instead of with some of the leaders of the church. This thoughtlessness on my part provided an opportunity for rumors to begin spreading in the congregation. In addition, some of the leaders became suspicious when they heard about my changes secondhand. For my part, I had to confide in someone while I was undergoing this trauma, and I dreaded making my views public since this was an irrevocable step.

Finally, I mustered my courage and revealed what had been happening in my life to the leaders of the church. I told them (with much trepidation) my conscience no longer permitted me to accept our charismatic practices as genuine manifestations of the Holy Spirit. Some of them were quite shocked, and all of us agreed we had a very grave situation on our hands. The question was, what course of action should we take?

It was decided I should first present my case to the leaders as representatives of the congregation. They honestly wanted to know why my views had changed, and they desired to understand my position. So we decided to study the Bible together as long

as it would take to come to a clear understanding of the issues involved. Then, if I
could adequately justify my position in their
eyes, I would take my case to the congregation. In the meantime, we declared a mora-
torium on the public use of charismatic gifts
and solicited the church's prayers.

As we began meeting together, not
one person on the council agreed with my
position, although some were sympathetic.
And at first no one was in the mood for com-
promise. And so week after week I presented
my case in great detail. I told them about the
burden of the prophets and of my reserva-
tions concerning tongues. I explained that
our experiences of these gifts did not favor-
ably compare with their miraculous repre-
sentation in the Scriptures.

Throughout the course of our meetings there was a great deal of discussion. Although there were times when our discussion degenerated into arguments, for the
most part I felt that we were proceeding in
accordance with the fruit of the Spirit.
Gradually, they began to concede that many
of my arguments were weighty and deserved
careful consideration. In particular, my ex-
position of the nature of prophecy seemed to
have a powerful impact. I could see my colleagues were starting to question the authenticity of prophetic gifts in our church.

Meanwhile, as the council continued
to deliberate, the emotional climate of the

church grew very tense. Many were quite understandably grieved with me on account of my new convictions. And I suppose had I been in their shoes, I would have felt the same way. In their minds, not only were the gifts of the Spirit at stake, but also their vision of the church's future direction. To some, the withdrawal of these gifts from the church would be just the first step in a process that would ultimately result in the Lord removing our candlestick (Revelation 2:5). As they peered into the future one word filled the field of their vision, *Ichabod*—the glory has departed. And so their sense of duty placed them in the unpleasant position of opposing their pastor.

However, human nature being what it is, situations of this kind are rarely resolved without first sorely degenerating. Some of my charismatic brothers and sisters grew deeply bitter and began to resent me for what I represented. One member of the congregation told me that my preaching was no longer anointed by the Holy Spirit. In addition, I began to receive letters and phone calls from irate people not only from my church, but from other charismatic churches in the area as well. Perhaps only another pastor who has faced a similar situation would be able to appreciate the deep sorrow I felt. Well did Paul warn the church, "If you keep on biting and devouring each other, watch out or you will be destroyed by each other" (Galatians 5:15).

Go Tell It to Your Brethren

Ironically, the more bitter my opponents became, the more my colleagues on the council came to my defense, even if they were not fully persuaded my position was valid. And in the end, I believe one of the observations that finally pushed the council over to my position was that some who claimed to be Spirit-filled failed to manifest the Spirit's quintessential mark—love. And so Haman was hung on the gallows he had built for Mordecai.

Now the time had come to present my case to the church. I did this in a series of four sermons which, owing to my nervousness, were not destined to be numbered among my better homiletical efforts. By this time I was so drained of my resources, I simply explained my position in the faith that if it were God's will, He would bear witness to the truthfulness of my account.

After the series was completed, I was gratified to learn many of the people were persuaded my testimony was true. What surprised me most was that some people had already been entertaining the same kinds of questions in their own hearts. Yet, since it seems so unspiritual for someone who has received these gifts to subsequently question their validity, they suppressed their doubts and lived with unanswered questions. They were waiting for someone to answer the questions they did not even dare to ask. So, when I articulated my position it was readily received by many with a sense of great liberty and relief. One of the leaders on the council who had been firmly opposed to my views said that next to being saved, this was one of the most liberating experiences of his life.

And it seems that I was not the only one who was acquainted with the "burden of the prophets." Some people confided that they had secretly entertained misgivings about the origin of their prophecies for years. One person confessed, "My endeavors to speak on God's behalf amounted to two years of self-torture." Another said, "I remember going to church and almost enviously looking at others and wishing that I didn't have the burden of prophecy hanging over me. Once I even secretly prayed that God would take the gift of prophecy from me. Then I quickly repented for thinking such sinful thoughts."

The person who spoke these latter words was Laurie. Everyone in the church acknowledged that Laurie had the gift of prophecy. Indeed, if anyone had the gift of prophecy, Laurie did. But no one knew of the intense conflict she was experiencing in her heart. Laurie had moved away from the church shortly before the spiritual gifts crisis began. But her own struggles were brought to a head when she learned of the changes that the church was going through. After a friend sent her a copy of the four sermons that I had preached, she wrote me a letter and asked me straight out, "Do you believe that my prophecies were of the Lord?" I wrote back that at one time I did. But with love and firmness I said that I didn't think that any of us really had the gift of prophecy.

Subsequently, she wrote back and said, "Neil, you said what I had been waiting to hear for seven long years." She went on to say, "I cried with relief and regret. It was as if my soul were saying 'It's over—it's finally over. You don't have to prophesy any more.' I cried, too, because of how foolish I had been. I had a long tearful time in prayer."

Many other people expressed relief because, for them, tongues had ceased. Here, as with prophecy, there had been gnawing doubts. Some felt that their tongues were repetitious and unlike a real language. Many felt guilty because they were exhorted so often from the pulpit to use their "prayer language." The trouble was that for some, tongues seemed to be a meaningless experience. And so instead of questioning the authenticity of their gift, they had concluded they were sinful or unspiritual.

One member, Roy, said praying in tongues had not been an edifying experience for him. He explained, "I was led to believe there was more power in praying in tongues then there was in English. I was puzzled, though, because the Scriptures exhort us to make our requests known to God with thanksgiving. Often, after I had spent a season praying in tongues, I still felt heavy-laden. I did not have the feeling that I had cast all my cares upon the Lord. However, when I prayed in English, there was a sense of relief."

Another person confessed that the pleasant feelings which she experienced while speaking in tongues were the same kinds of sensations she experienced while chanting meaningless mantras when she was involved in Transcendental Meditation as a non-Christian.

Of course, not everyone agreed with me. Some who were not convinced either way "tabled" their experiences. Some remained charismatic but accepted the change with sadness and love for the sake of unity. I have great admiration for the sacrifices these good Christians made. Still others decided to leave on the grounds they could no longer in good conscience affiliate themselves with the church. I admired these people too, and they left with my blessing. But there were a few who left the church under the most disappointing and unpleasant circumstances. This was grievous for all to bear.

Throughout this crisis, God had given me the strength to cope with the emotional strain that was involved. But one evening at a prayer meeting, I experienced a sort of delayed-stress reaction. The meeting was somber because one of our deacons had left the church that day. As I watched my friends singing and praying, I felt strangely isolated, and there was a great weight upon my heart. The bitterness, the sorrow, and the stress of many months were conspiring together in my heart that night. Then, when prayer was routinely offered for the pastor, I could scarcely keep from bursting into tears. To avoid an embarrassing situation, I excused myself from the meeting. And as I drove home alone that night, I found release in a flood of tears.

Those were difficult days for all of us at Word of Life Church. What changes we went through! At times, we couldn't help but wonder what the future would hold. Some members saw this transition as a tragic move away from a work established by the Holy Spirit. But for many of us it was the beginning of a new life in the Spirit, and of a more profound understanding of the meaning of spirituality. We placed our trust in Him who said, "Behold, I will do something new."

Epilogue

If there is one word that best describes the struggles—the fears within and the conflicts without—it is disillusionment. For a time it hung over my head like a dark cloud. So much that I had believed in, so much that I had cherished, so much of my past spiritual history was shattered. The transition from shadow to substance is natural and wholesome. But to reverse the process, to discover that so much that you

Epilogue

thought was substantial is a shadow—a mere mirage—is devastating.

Fortunately, I recognized that this was all part of a healthy process. To be disillusioned presupposes the existence of an illusion. By all means then, let that which is illusory fade away. The thing to do is not to be swept away by emotional self-indulgence and pity, but rather to rebuild your life on a more solid foundation. Let the pain of disillusionment call you to consecrate yourself with all your might to a new and better vision. That's the cure of disillusionment.

Isaiah, speaking of Israel's future, said, "The mirage shall become a pool, and the thirsty ground springs of water" (Isaiah 35:7 Amplified). To a desert people, a people well-acquainted with the "howling wilderness," there is nothing as cruel as a mirage. But the prophet foresees a day when illusions, so disappointing to those who thirst, will become pools of refreshing water. May there not come a similar moment in our lives as well? A time when the mirage becomes a pool and living water springs forth from our innermost being?

Since my journey from the mirage to the pool, the words of the familiar hymn have taken on a new significance for me:

> How firm a foundation, ye saints of
> the Lord

Epilogue

Is laid for your faith in His excellent
  Word!
What more can He say than to you He
  hath said,
To you who for refuge to Jesus have
  fled?

There you have the pool that can never dis-
appoint—His excellent Word. There are no
floods so mighty, no winds so strong, that
they can shake the house that is built on
that firm foundation. What more can He
say? What more do we need?